A Chymicall Treatise

of the Ancient and highly illuminated
Philosopher, Devine and Physitian,

Arnoldus de Nova Villa

who lived Foure hundred years agoe, never seene in
print before, but now by a Lover of the Spagyrick art
made publick for the use of Learners,
printed in the year 1611.

Here Beginns
Mr. Arnold de Nova Villa's Treatise.

He speakes to his Scholars thus, Know my deare Sonne that this is a Booke of the Secrets of nature, and I shall devide it into six parts. In the first discourse what the stone is, secondly why the Stone is naturall, thirdly why the Stone is animal like our blood, fourthly why it is called herball or Radicall, fifthly I'll relate its true and constant preparation, and sixtly I shall truly and without lies give you an account of the augmentaion of our growing stone, to the end that fooles may bee derided, and wise and understanding men taught. This art is nothing else but a knowing of the secret and hid things of naturall masterrs and Lovers of the naturall art and wisdome, therefore no body should approach to this art, unlesse he has heard before some Logick, which teaches to distinguish truth from falsehood, and withall the naturall art which teaches the things of nature, and the property of the elements, otherwise he troubles his minde and body and life in vaine, it is a Stone and no Stone, and is found by every body in plane fields, on Mountaines, and in the water, and is called Albida, heerein all physitians agree, for they say that Albida is called Rebio, they name it in hid and secret words, because they perfectly understand the materiam, some say it is blood, others say it is mans hair, others say it is eggs, which has made many fooles and unwise men, that understand no more then the letter, and the meere sound of words, seeke this art in blood, in eggs, in hair, in the Gaull, in Allum , in salt, but they have found nothing for they did not rightly understand the sayings of naturalists, who spake their words in hid language, should they have spoken out plainly, they would have done very ill for divers reason, for all men would have used this art and the whole world would have been spoiled, and all agriculture perisht; seeing it is so that a man must give an account of his workes, I desire god, that he would give me reason, and wisdome, and direct me how I may estrange or conceale this noble art from fooles, which made me say what this stone is; Know my sonne that our Stone as Hermes speakes is in a living thing, out of which saying the true attempt of this art may bee knowne, and because of this saying some according to their folly have sought this stone in beasts, in herbs, in Allum, but they have remained fooles; now I'll tell you what our stone is, Sol, Luna, Azoth, now there are three stones and they are dead upon earth, and end the thing afore in Lunam by the carefull understanding and preparation of man; out of this stone is made true gold and silver the same with naturall; the Scholar sayd how can this bee, for the philosophers say that art is weaker then nature, and you say, out of that stone is made gold and Silver the same with naturall. The Master answerr'd wee doe not make it, as nature makes it, but we helpe nature with our art, in which respect it is naturall and not artificiall; there are three things in the naturall art and wisdome as Hermes says, when the Stone is in a thing that has a Soule, as the Soule is spirituall when it goes away in Smoak, for which cause its call'd a fugitive servant, and a finite Spirit, for in the world there is no other spirit to this art, and it is of an Ayry nature, which is a sign of perfection, and that it is not in Salt or Allum; he is not wise that seekes in a thing what is not in it, and because neither gold nor Silver is in Allum or Salt, wee must not seek them there but in such things where gold and silver is to bee found.

But that our Stone is not in beasts, heare how Hermes saith. All things are made according to their nature. Out of man another man is made, and out of a living creature another living Creature is produced, and one thing produceth another like it selfe. How then can the medicine helpe man, it being not fit for man? The Master answeres thus, Understand the Sayings of Wise men. The Medicines which are given to man doe not make

5

man, but drive away his distempers, and so it is here. Our Medicine given to him to whom wee ought to give it, makes true gold and Silver which is subject to no defect, and changes the man into the Woman, and the Woman into the man, and the man into an angell; how can that bee saith the Scholar? Thou hast heard it in the preparation only, perceive well the words of the Naturalists and bee wise and not unwise, it being necessary that our Stone must bee of an incombustible nature and matter it is evident, that it is not found in salt, or animals, or any of the other mentioned, but that Mercury is alone an incombustible spirit, and therefore necessarily must bee an object of our science; so then it is manifest what the Stone is, and how much, and how it is not. Know my Son, that our Stone is naturall, for many reasons; first it is naturall because nature in the like manner makes man and woman as the wise may know, but the unwise doth not understand this. Secondly it is called naturall by Hermes the father of all Naturalists, a man who is to bee beleived. Thirdly the medicine is found naturally, the things which are under the Circle of the Moone being foure elements. And therefore our Stone is joyned together by the Foure elements, and among the Foure elements one is cold, another drye, some warme, some moist. The Scholar here saith, Then our Stone is cold, moist, dry and hot. The Master answeres: Understand plainly. The Seven planets are Stones. Mercury is warm and dry because of the Sunne, cold and moist because of the Moone, for he is of the nature of water, of aire, of earth and of Fire. Therefore he is as the thing to which you joined him, Good with the good, and bad with the bad, which makes Aristotle say, when thou hast Water out of the aire, and aire out of the fire, and fire out of the earth (open thy eares and understand the sayings of the wise) Then thou hast the whole Art.

Know my sonne that our Stone is animal-like. The Scholar saith, what is the reason of this? The Master replyes, because hee hath a Spirit, and therefore a soul which makes it animal-like. The Scholar: how hath it a Soule? The Master: dost not thou know that there are Foure Spirits, Sulphur, Arcenicum, Salmoniac, and Mercurius, you see it is under the number of these Foure spirits and therefore it is a Spirit, and the Soule, and because it is a Soule it must needs bee animal-like, for animals have soules, here abouts marke well as I have told thee of spirits and of the Soule and of the animal-like to the animal-like, this is the reason why our Stone is animal-like, and Hermes in Libro Senator saith, our Stone is of a thing that hath a Soule that is of a Spirit or fugitive thing, but the fooles and unwise men who thought, as some yet think that it is in beasts, finde and loose tyme and labour and spoil both their bodies and goods. The Scholar sayes: why is our Stone blood? Because

Arcaglaus sayes take the Stone which the ancients bid you take and rub him so long till he be rub'd to blood, that is, till he become red, and because of the rednesse he is called blood, and when our Stone becomes red, then he has in him the nature of fire, and out of it all secrets may be drawn, mark and perceive what I say, and thou wilt have the whole art, fools who thought that he was blood, did labour in blood and found nothing, for things are made according to their nature. The naturall Master says: make out of the Stone flesh and blood, that he may bee red and thou wilt have the whole art, Make of the Milk that is of white Stone flesh and blood, that it may bee white like milke and may flow. The Scholar saith: how is this stone made white, and how is it made red? The Master answeres, Take the Stone and rubb him with blood, and it will bee red, However I declare the Art to thee otherwise, and clearer. Take the small and inconsiderable and rub it with the most amiable and the best, and it will be made red by the help of the Fire, Observe here that the fire causes them to joyne and purgeth them, and adornes them. But the unwise, who perceive not the Speeches of the Naturall Masters, try the art according to the outward Letter, and finde nothing and then cry It's a Lye, and the art is false, for wee have tryed it and found nothing. Thus they despaire, and raile against the books and the Art. The Scholar saith, why is this Stone Herball? The Master answers:

because as the herbe hath a moveable soule, so our stone hath a Soule, for Hermes saith our Stone is of a thing having a Soule, but the unwise thought it was in herbs yet did not finde it there, and so have renounced the art. Some say that Mercury should bee compounded or coagulated with the herbs and so have sought him in the herbs and found nothing, Yet this I doe not say as if the Mercurius could not bee compounded or coagulated with the herbs, but I say that the coagulation is good for nothing, and when they have thus coagulated him, they think they have done great matters, yet have done nothing that's worth anything, nor finished any thing; it being inconstant they talke, I can coagulate the Mercurius, but they might rather say, I can spoile the Mercurius. And what is it that Mercurius is to bee coagulated with? They make him of herbes, and make so fragil, that he is worth nothing. Mercurius, if hee bee rightly coagulated hee must bee as heavy in weight as gold though hee bee white in colour, for the Whitenesse is a Signe of perfection. This done, there needs no more but only to give him the color, and so it is gold. The Scholar saith, why is our Stone called the red Servant? The Master answeres: because hee soon turnes red. The Scholar: why doe the philosophers say, that Mercury doth not dye, unlesse it be killed with its Brother? The Master: Hermes saith That the Dragon dyes not, unlesse you kill him with its Brother the Sun, or Sister the Moone. Therefore saith Avicenna, Make the blind to see, and the seeing blind, and thou wilt have the Art. Another saith, in the Herball Stone are Haire, Blood, Eggs, and this hee said to shew in these words, the Foure Elements, beleeve not mee but the naturall philosophers, who may bee beleeved, nor give an credit to common foolish recipes. For those that have made recipes found nothing of this art, but they had some books of the philosophers, who speake in riddles of this art (For they framed these bookes with such hid words as with allum and Salt, and with other things unintelligible to the simple, though intelligible enough to the prudent) that they have deceived the whole world. I saw a Monck who had laboured in this Art very neere twenty yeares, and could finde nothing notwithstanding of this, however like a base raskall hee made a booke which hee called, The Flowers of Paradise, in which were above 100 recipes, and this booke he suffered to come into every man's hand, and by these meanes much people was deceived, for hee was a Coxcomb and knew nothing.

In this Chapter I will teach the preparation of the Philosophers Stone, but the way of its preparation which I know, I have not of myselfe, but a part of this Labor, I have of one of my brethren, and a part of a German Moncke. Therefor I desire God that he take away from mee the sin of envy, that I may bring every body into the way of truth. In the beginning of this labour, I'll say, that the most excellent Hermes teaches the way in plain words to rationall men, but in occult and hid speeches to the unwise and fools. I say that the father son and holy ghost are one, and yet three, so speaking of our Stone I say three are one, and yet are divided. Mark well, the World was lost by a Woman, therefore necessarily must it bee restored by a Woman. Take therefore the mother very pure and lay her into a bed with the Servant, and putt them up close into a Prison, till they bee purified of their sins, and shee'le beare a son, which will bee a blessing to all people. Signes have been manifested in the sun and in the moone. Then take the son and beate him that he may be punished and its pride may come down, and he forsake his pride, and abide in humility. Therefore, saith Geber, out of Mercury everything is made. The same Chapter saith further, The common Sulphur is found in Sol and Luna, in Mercury more fugitive, in the body water. And the same in another chapter saith, Afterward the Tincture becomes Water, that it may become better in its nature. Therefore take the punished son and lay him into a bed and there hee'le begin to delight himselfe, then take him and give him to the Jewes to bee crucified. Being crucifyed hee growes pale, then take him, and turne him, and if you cannot see him well, you take away the vaile from the Temple, whereupon a great earth quake ariseth and you'le see various changes, and hee'le leape up and downe because of his great

11

tortures, then hee'le fall downe; therefore stirr him below more, and hee'le give up the ghost. Thus all necessary things are accomplished, and many Workmen have erred in this.

The Scholar said, these words I understand not. The Master answered, I must necessarily hide the Secrets of Secrets of the naturall art, as other Natural Masters have done, for it is not with this art as it is with others. Hence it is said, whatsoever is written, is written for our Learning, that through patience and comfort of the holy ghost, wee may have the Scripture. Amen.

I came one day into a great Master's house to recreate my selfe with him in this art for sport, yet with magisteriall words, and I sat at his right side; There were two men with him. The one I knew, but the other I did not know. These two began to speake of this art, neither being ashamed of mee, nor taking any care of mee. Then understood I by their speeches that which I had sought a great while. Yet did they wonder what I sought there and were amazed at the speech, which they had had together. Then turned the honest old man his face towards mee and said, The wise and prudent Mercurius (to speake the common way) is comprehended in these words. Take leade and whatsoever is like lead, and take Azoth. This is the right ordering of the art, which the Egyptians have acknowledged and that's their riddle, their reason, their vertue, and their meeknesse. Here are foure things, two are manifest which hee named the lead, and that which is like lead. Then said one of the men, how many are the things, to which the other said, there are foure, and said moreover: These art words of the prudent and wise, and have a darke obscurity in them, and are taken out of the apparent sentences of the wise. Then the one asked, how is this? to which the other answering said the wise man understands but two. The one asked againe, which are they two? The man answered and said, The hidden thing after this hee adds two words and they signifie foure, and foure signifie but two, and hee changed the words of the wise before mentioned and said foure. And the wise men say but two. Then he answered and said as it was said before, In these words is a hidden obscurity and they are taken out of the illustrious sayings of the wise. Hereby meanes the Master nothing else then that out of the foure things two should bee set together, man and wife. And having thus used diverse words among the rest he said, Take Fire and water, and mingle these two together, and there will bee one thing out of it. After this he said, Take Lead and that which resembles lead, and he changed these words and said, Take Azoth and that which resembles Azoth; with such hidden words doe they hide their words to all unwise men. Perceive therefore and trust God, that thou mayst perceive the better the aforesaid saying of the wise. Of this I'll give thee an example when the Master saith, Take Lead, according to a philosophicall sense or meaning. The word lead is a manly name and word, and so one of the number of the names of men. Hereby mayst thou truly know the name of the man. And he saith further, That which resembles lead, that is, that which resembles the man. So hee hides the name of the Woman, and the reason why he mentions the man's name first is because shee is of him, and not hee of her. Therefore said the master, That which resembles Lead. After this one said, Take Azoth and that which resembles Azoth. The Masters hereby meane the wife. Here he names the Woman, and mentions not the name of the man, for hee had named him before in the beginning of these words, where he saith, Take Adam and what resembles Adam. Afterwards hee changeth this Speeche againe, to make it more occult to him that is not altogether wise, and said, Take Eva, and what resembles Eva, here thou namest Eva and not the man, and this thou doest, because thou didst begin in the first speech with the man. That these Speeches doe not at all hinder a wise man in his reason, but make him more ingenious, and more intelligent.

When they had talk'd together a great while, they began againe in a great feare another way and language. Mingle the warm with the cold, for so an equall mixture will arise out of it, which is neither warme nor cold, and mix the moist with the dry,

and you'le have an equall mixture, which is neither
moist nor dry. The Speech now uttered, is manifest
from Foure things, and out of these foure are
numbered and terminated Man and Wife. The man
is hot and dry, the wife cold and moist, but when
they come together, and unite themselves
naturally, there is made an equall mixture of the
warme and the cold, of the moist with the dry. And
of this a wise Philosopher doth not doubt, and the
artificiall conjunction cannot bee unlesse the things
belonging thereunto be totally prepared, every one
according to its kind. For as Joseph saith, Mix
together fire and water, and there will be two, Mix
together aire and earth, and there will bee foure,
Afterward of foure make one, then thou art come to
what thou wouldst bee att. And when this is done
make out of that body a non-corpus, that is a Spirit,
as out of the non-corpus or Spirit make a body
againe, which may bee constant on the fire, and not
remove any way from it. Already, thou hast
comprehended the Wisdom. Doe in this as Joseph
hath said. Before thou beginnest the labour of this
Artificiall treasure which is true, prepare all
things, each in their kind and nature, begin thence
to the end, and when thou hast done this thou hast
made a water which is warme and not warm, cold
and not cold, moist and not moist, dry and not dry
according to its nature, and it is fixed, that it
cannot fly, and it is the thing which reveales and

opens to thee the tincture, and if it were not for this Artificiall water, all hope would bee in vaine.

When the Masters speake here and there, they still come to this Noble water. The reason is because that water is a medium between the contrary things, this comes from thence, and it is water and no water, fire and no fire, aire and no aire, earth and no earth. Because then it is and is not, according to its Noble Nature it is a right medium betweene the unlimited Elements. This Noble water is the beginning, middle and end of this Noble art, perceive this speech well together with the former. For the Masters speake commonly one thing, and meane it in another sense, and where they spake most hiddenly and most profoundly, there they doe mean it most simply, and where they speake most plainly and openly then they doe hide most this divine and Noble art. Out of this speech and sentences it is manifest, that this art may bee taught with all its Secretes in a few words, nor will any man be found in time to come, that will say so much in writing as is said here, unlesse one should show it to the other with hand and mouth and reveal'd and open'd all to him, for the philosophers have unwillingly discovered this amiable truth, and have reserv'd it to themselves and taken it with them downe to the Grave; and what in other Bookes is taught by examples and circumstances, that is express'd here cleerely, and thus this Noble Art is written by me truly and sincerely.

Therefore that my name and memory may for ever remaine upon the earth, I have written this small booke and made it by the help of the Holy Ghost, for all Posterities and Children of God and of this Art.

One time I sate alone in my Chamber with my Wife, and read the Bookes of the ancient deceased philosophers, and those also that have liv'd in my time, and there I found written something of Alkabrith and Zandorit, and of other strange words and things whereby one may turne every man from the right way, and he that matters it looses his time, goods and substance and last his health, and miserably robbs himselfe of life; and that thou mayest believe me the better I tell the whole truth, that no man can attain unto this art unlesse he retires from the world and converses with his equalls, and joyn himself to them, and though every one sayes that hee reveals it, yet however all hide it as thou seest by me that I doe reveale it, but not to the unwise and foolish; and if I truly discover this divine art, my booke will bee so profitable to them, that the bookes of wise men and my words will bee the same, my words theirs, and theirs mine; not that I would steale their words from them and make them mine owne, this would be unjust, but only my meaning agrees with theirs, and theirs againe with me. Therefore whosoever

17

will finde out the Secrets of this Art, let him read this booke and understanding. And why? because this booke is cleere and known to understanding men and to those that observe carefully and reade with attention in it, but to the unwise and unexpert, and those that are not diligent it must needs bee hidd as it is from children. Know then, that there art many who labour hard in the preparation of Sulphur, and in the Sublimation of Arsenicum, which art combustible and corruptible. These men only looke to the words which they reade or heare, and not to the hidden sense that is in those words. For truly the Sulphur, Arsenicum, Auripigment, Zandorit, Vibrick, Mercurius, Salt, Saltpeter, Sala Pculi, Salmiac and Allum signifie in this Noble art in truth nothing but water, and the making white the Philosophers talk of, is nothing else but the purification of the Water that it may bee clearer and purer, and by the sublimation or exaltation understand nothing else, but the ascension of the vapour from the water in the Cucurbit below and above in the Alembick and againe through the Canales Laterales in the Cucurbit, and againe through the Canales laterales; and by the washing understand The Bodies changing into water so long till out of the Water a part in it of the manifold vapours ascends, and falling downe againe are coagulated and consolidated that it may never rise againe, and the reason hereof is because the corporeal Spirit in the

Spirituall and the Spirituall againe in the corporeal
has mixed and soaked it selfe, and because the
Spirituall Spirit is stronger than the Corporeall
Spirit, they both are vapourous and ellevate
themselves in the height of the allembick; but when
the corporeall Spirit overcomes the Spirituall he
must necessarily remaine with him at the bottome
in the Cucurbit, and when they have united
themselves the Spirituall Ghost which is
penetrable makes the corporeall Spirit together
with himself penetrable and permeable, for the
corporeall Spirit has in him the tincture, that is,
the red and white colour, and with all the Spirituall
Spirit leads the corporeall in and without
hinderance just as a man does goe through a house
with an open doore, and is not spied by any, so it is
here; but this cannot be unlesse the body that will
draw the Spirit out of the man, bee totally cleansed
from all impurity, and thereby the Leprosie of the
whole from the whole be perceived. Understand
this, that is, that ashes be drawne and made, for
thus the bodies are deprived of lustiness and
moistness, and so the body may first become
spirituall, when the body is turned to ashes
according to its highest purification, and out of
those ashes be made a Lixevium, in that waterish
nature the body becomes spirituall; and understand
this secret how the body has the ashes in it, and in
the ashes is the Stone, and the Stone is the Spirit,
and in the Spirit there is the tincture or colour, and

in the tincture the Soul, and the Soul had in her a
fiery permeation, and leads with her the colour in
the body; and he that does not understand how he
shall begin this, how will he come to the middle, or
to the end, therefore thus speake all masters: it is
one body, and yet there are many bodies, and those
many are no more then one body, this understand
allso it is one body because it is not beaten as soone
as it is turned into ashes, each singular dust is a
singular body and when the ashes are turned into
water it is a water and no water and may with
artificiall industry be returned into a body, but
before this the body must often rest in the belly of
the wind under the height of the heavens; and
therefore the Masters say it is a Stone, and
resembles the Eagles Stone for the Eagles Stone is
such a Stone that in his belly there is another
Stone, and if you will pull it out from thence, you
must turne the Stone into Ashes, and out of the
ashes there is first another Stone made, and when
that Stone does sweat right, its owne Water is
made of it, and when he has well sweated, he
drincks the Sweaty Water againe into him, and flys
afterwards up and downe, and from the great
motion which he does force up above his Mass in
the aire, the water becomes of itself againe a Stone,
and by the paraphrase of the Eagle, understand the
evaporation of the vaporous spirit, and by their
redescention understand the heavy falling downe of
the body; yet there are many who call the aforesaid

ashes a sowre masse or a Leaven, but they know not their water, that the corporeall nature attracts the coagulated nature out of those ashes.

Moreover says Master Joseph their Spirit is the fusion of both bodies, by this he does not meane the dissolutions of the bodyes on the fire, but he meanes that they should bee turned into Mercury, and that out of the Mercury the flowers should be extracted, and this is the Stone whereof Aristotle spoke to his King, did men know what a great Treasure they had in Saturnus they would not give it for a small summe of Money, but they would make so much gain by it, that one might bring the whole World into his Subjection; and another Master said, take the things as they come out of their treasury, and lift them up in the highest mountains, and humble them again from the highest mountains to their roots, these are the wisest words which he has spoken openly without all envy and without any secrecy, and afterward hee hath not named the things he meant, in the heighth of the Mountaines and by the roots. For as in Mountaines naturall gold is made, and in the ground, so in this art, our gold is made in the heighth of the Alembick, and in the roote that is in the Cucurbit. And this is a cleanly similitude which may easily be perceived, and hereby you may understand, when the Master speake of the highe mountaines or the deepe grounds that they doe not meane the heads of men or their feete, so when they speake of haire, and of blood, they only understand the resemblance of them. Therefore many men are deceived, which looke after the literall sense and seeke it where it is not to bee found. For this Art is so noble that it must be sought and found out in it selfe, and no thing like to it. As out of a man is made another man, so out of one Noble Mettall is made another Mettall, and there is no transmutation, as some idle and simple men thinke. Who doth not mollify and harden againe doth erre, therefore make the earth black, and separate her Soule from her, and the water, after that make it white that it may become as a naked Sword and when it growes white, give it to the Covetous fire so long till it growes large, and doth not fly away; Hee that can doe this may well be called happy and exalted in this World, and let him doe it in the love of God and in his feare. Amen.

The first word in this great work is the bodies transmutation into Mercury and this the Philosophers have called a dissolution. And this Artificiall and ingenious dissolving is the bullwark of this art. Hence saith Rosarey, Unlesse you dissolve the bodies, Your Labor is in vaine. Therefore the dissolving of Philosophers is not a drinking in but the bodies transmutation into water. Nor is it called a Philosophical dissolving unlesse it becomes cleere as Mercury, so thou wilt have an element, which is the water.

The second word is that it be purified and filled with its terra; of this speakes Morienus, let the earth bee filled with its water, and let it bee cleansed with it, and when it is purified on both sides it ends the whole art. Aristotle sayes in generall, put the dry to the moist, the dry is the terra, the moist is the water, thus thou hast earth and water each by it self, and the earth is purified with the water, and when they are cleansed one with the other, thou hast Colours cleerer then before, therefore saies Rosarius in generall, if one by day sees many starrs in the heavens, the sunne is hindered of its Lustre by moon, and when that does vanish the Sunn shines clearer then before.

The third word, that the water does lift itself in vapours which is condensed and coagulated of the earth, and thick, that is that it makes it selfe spirituall in the aire, and so thou hast Water, earth and aire, and while it hurvers in the aire Archelaous calls it the great Master Hermeses bird by way of similitude; therefore sayes Alberius, make him white, or white him with the nimblenesse of the fire, so long till out of him arises the spirit which is called Hermeses bird, so the earth will remaine cinerated in the ground which is of a fiery nature, so thou hast Foure elements in the earth which did remaine in the ground, and it is the fire; hence Morienus: the Earth which remaines in the ground, thou must not at all despise nor villify, understand the earth of the body, and that same earth is the right end of the permanent and constant things, after that with a good water thou must annoint and errigate the Leaven, and the Leaven is called by the Philosophers a Soul; they call also the prepared body a Leaven, for as a Leaven does make other bread sowre, so does this thing, and I tell thee freely, that there is no other Leaven but Gold and Silver, of necessity must the Leaven bee Leavened in the body, for the Leaven is the Soule of the body, and therefore says Morienus: Unlesse you purify the unclean body, and create in him a new soule, you have perceived Lesse then nothing in this art; likewise says Arnuldus, the spirit changes into the body, and cleanses and eterniseth him, about this the Spirit does tye himself, and the clear permeations of the Soul which here is mentioned is a Leaven, and rejoyces with the body, because it has cleansed it selfe with him and now the nature is changed so that the grosser things stay behind there; says Aschanos in Turba Philosophorum, the Spirit is not joyned to the body unlesse before it bee totally purified from all uncleanesse, but in the conjunction, the greatest miracles are made evident, for there are seen all the colours that a man can think of; and when the colours beginn to bee lighter and lighter so that thou seest sometimes onely as it were a little spark and beginns to rejoyce therein from thy heart and Soul, then take heed, for our basilisk prepares himself who kills

24

men more for joy, which they conceive from him then for his poyson, for his poyson lasts but a moment, that is when the supreme power or the Quintessence of the elements does discover it self in so many wayes and colours, and the last is done in a Moment; when this is done thou seest the sun and Moone shine lovely in the heaven of his owne water, and begins to rejoyce but then goe away lest thou loosest thy life for joy, and thus the imperfect body is coloured with his best colours because of the power of the heaven, and the heaven is the soul, and the Spirit is with the help of the soul joyned to the body, and are tyed one with the other, and the body is changed to the colour of the Leaven and becomes eternally good; out of the Words prescribed and said any understanding man may know that the philosophers in dark and hidden wordes have hidde the whole art, for they say our Stone is of Foure elements, and that's a great truth, for they have compar'd them with Foure elements whereof Wee have said enough, and one may know the elements by the coloures, he that knowes it, and is acquainted with it; some Philosophers have said that our Stone is of a body, of a soul, and of a Spirit, and they have said true, and wee doe yeild, and they give to the perfect body what he had not before, and it brings him into a better spirit; the Soul brings into the imperfect body a constant spirit, which is not at all fugitive before the Aire, and therefore it keeps its colour and weight unchangeably and the more you drive it the more noble it becomes both in colour and weight. Some also say unless you change the bodies into no bodies, and the nobodies againe into bodies, you are not come yet to the right art, for the body becomes first an aqua Mercury incorporal and afterwards the Water and the Spirit in the changing and so both become one body; some also say change the natures quite and cleane and you will finde what you seeke; and that's true, for we make of that which is grosse a subtle and quick thing, and of a body we make water, and of that which is moist we make a dry thing, of the water we make the earth, and thus wee change the true natures and make of that which is corporall a spirituall thing and of a Spirituall a corporall thing, and wee make that which is above like that which is below, and that which is below like that which is above, the Spirit is turned to a body, and the body to a Spirit; and therefore its said in the beginning, the Word was a Spirit, and that word the Spirit was with God, that is with himselfe, and God was that word, he himself was the Spirit, and the word the Spirit was made flesh, the Spirit has assumed the true body, and so that above became true as that below, the Spirit has become a mettallick in the body, and that which was below, that is, the body, is become mettallicke with the Spirit; and thus it is well known that our Stone is out of the elements and it is a body, a soul, a spirit, and not two spirits, one soul and not two soules; and the saying of Philosophers is true who say our Stone is made but of one thing, and therein they have said very true, for it is made only of water. And in the water and out of the water our whole art hath an end, for it dissolves the bodies with the dissolution aforementioned; not with such a dissolution as unwise men fancy, that our Stone should be changed into Water, but it's dissolved with the true naturall dissolution, so that he is changed into such a water as it was from the beginning before it was a body, and that very water incinerates and turnes the body again to earth into ashes, and makes them penetrable, and does whiten and purifie them, as Morienus says: Azoth and the fire purifies Latonem, and take all his darknesse away, Laton an impure body set together of Gold and Silver, Azoth and Mercury, and that two distinct bodies joyn the fire and Azoth together when they are ready as is said before, that no attempt against the fire or other attempts can part them, one from the other, and that same water does not sublimate neither does it exalt it self with a sublimation of fooles or exaltation as they imagine, but with the wise and understanding sublimation or exaltation; for our sublimation is making a noble thing out of an ignoble, therefore fooles take the shaved bodies and make them ascend by the heat of the fire, and mingle them with an impure spirit, as with Arsenick and Salmiack, and they make a Strong fire under it whereby the bodies ascend with the Spirit, and then they say now are the bodies sublimated; whereas they are quite Killed, for why they finde the bodies impure therefore observe that our Sublimation is not driving on and ascending, but the making of a dry thing and corrupted a sound one, a great and high one, and changing it into another nature, and making on a suddain sublime vapours, and all this does our Water together; and so understand our Sublimation and not otherwise, and take heed of the Sublimation of fooles, wherewith many are deceived; marke our water at first kills and makes alive again, and it makes white the black colour, when it's changed to earth, after that innumerable colours reflect from the whitenesse and all the colours last end is the white, for at last it turnes white; some call the Stone lead, as Gigill speakes, in our lead is the whole art, and if our lead be impure our stone is also impure, while he lyes in his mothers womb; O did the Lead Mongers know the vertue of Lead, they would not part with it for so small a price; some call our stone Cheife Copper or Clock minerall as Eximius speakes in generall. Know this all wee that seeke this art, that no tincture is made without this cheife Copper or Clock Minerall, and thus they have given it innumerable names, and yet meane no more but one thing, and this they have done for this reason, that fooles should not finde it out, for they have named it with all manner of names that can bee named, yet they have meant but one thing; and it is no more but one thing, to witt the Philosophycall water. Our art is also compared to man making. The first is the deprivation of its chastity, the second is the conception, the third is the being with childe, the fourth is the birth it selfe, and the fifth is the bringing up of the child borne; understand also these words, our Son that comes from the privation of chastity is Mercury, for he is drawn out of a perfect body so there remaines an earth the mother of Foure elements, and when the earth begins to take somewhat in of Mercury, it's call'd unchastity, but when the man lyes with the wife it's called conception, which without the Mercury is wrought in the earth; this is what the Philosophers say, our Art is nothing else but that the man lyes with his wife, and that they mingle one with the other, so that the Water governes and has the Mastery, and that the Mercury bee more then the Earth, and so earth encreases and augments; but when the earth becomes a wife she is with Child, after that the ferment is added to the imperfect prepared body as is said before, so long till it becomes something in colour and in sight and that's called the birth; so then our Stone is born, for the Philosophers call him King and say thus, honour your King who comes from the fire crowned with a double crown, bow the knees before him when he comes to his perfect alterr, for the sun is his father and the

Moone his Mother, the perfect body is Luna, the perfect body is gold; at last followes the nourishment whereby he is nourisht with a great nourishment, he is nourisht with his owne Milke, with the Seed in the beginning he is fed, to wit with Mercury, till he hath drunk enough of the Mercury. Beloved sonns by these things which are told you, You may easily perceive the darke and hidden worke of the Phylosophers and by that you may know that they all runne one way and upon one straine, and that our art is nothing else but what has beene said before, the dissolution of bodies and changing of their first matter, how it's made earth and how it becomes a light and spirituous in the aire with distilling it because of the moistnesse which is in it; thus it becomes lusty in vapours, and the earth remaines below incinerated and is of a fiery nature, thus you have truly the totall changing of things and the mingling of the Soul with the body and with the Spirit, and it assumes such a Spirituall and powerfull increase that humane reason cannot fathome it, the highest be praised and blessed for it for evermore.

Now will I in the name of God make manifest the practice and the very sense of the Philosophers how one shall perfect that Ellixir, that is the augmentation of the true tincture and of Silver and Gold only out of the Mercury of the Sages, or the minerall Mercury and in all copper bodies which fall short of perfection, insomuch that they become

30

perfect into a perfect Luna and gold above the naturall, which is not that common Mercury, call'd by the Philosophers prima materia, waterish hot moist and cold, an element, a constant water, a Spirit, a body, a swimming smoake, a blessed water, a water of the wise, a vinegar of Philosophers, a dew of Heaven, virgin Milke, a corporeal Mercury, besides others innumerable names whereby he is called in the Bookes of the Philosophers; allthough these names sound variously, yet they signifie but one thing, to witt the aforesaid Mercurium Philosophorum, for out of him, and in him and by him only are sought all the vertues of the whole art of Alchimy, and of the red and white tincture, Q and R.

Therefore saith Geber, without Mercury the art is not perfected. It is a thing, a Stone, a Medicine in which lyes the art, unto which no outward thing is to be applyed, only in the preparation the remaining or superfluous part is to bee taken of. Therefore in that and out of that a man may finde all things, needfull to this art. For it kills it selfe and revives it self, makes it selfe hard, makes it selfe weake, makes it self black white and red. And the same master in his discourse sayeth. Wee add no externall thing because of the gold and silver, for these are called not internall things, which are to bee adjoyned to the Mercury, For they are two Fellow Helpers whereby the whole work of the art is perfected. And another Philosopher saith, It is a thing, whereby many have beene undone, as a whole multitude was for one mans sake.

The Mercury is also called a naturall root of a high Tree out of which innumerable branches grow, and its call'd the knowne stone of the philosophers, and in the Bookes of Philosophers the first operation. To the perfection of the aforementioned Stone or Elixir belongs a Sublimation or exaltation which must bee brought to purity. And this I shall hereafter without the least covering make manifest. But you must note that this sublimation is nothing lesse than a purification, for hereby all remaining drosse that was in the Mercury is purged away, thus this sublimation the inconstant particles are lifted up from the constant, for the inconstant ascend and the constant remaine below at the bottome, yet in the operation the inconstant become in part constant and it's particularly to bee noted. Hee that rightly sublimates our Mercury, hee hath perfected the whole art, For Master Geber saith, The whole perfection is in the sublimation in the vessel, and in the ordering of the fire, for in the already mentioned sublimation are comprehended all other particulars, which belong to our art and labour, as sublimating, dissolving, ascending, descending, cooling, mollifying, purifying, and perpetuating, washing and colouring on red and white. All is done in a vessel in order in an oven, whereof the Masters of nature have written much that the art was not to bee perfected constantly, on purpose, that the unwise might reach to it, but to the just and to the godly it becomes profitable both here and hereafter.

Now make it thus. Take in the name of God the aforementioned Mercury or the naturall Water, the first matter of the Sages, Take of it as much as you will, and putt it into its vessell which must be pure, cleare, and cleane, and Seale it well above with the Sigills Hermetis, that the Mercury may not come out above, and sett it in its prepared place, that it may have a moderate heate every moment for a month. The naturall master saith That it may have its place warme whereby it works it self up and downe, so long til it ascend no more in the glasse, and begins to bee colle at the bottome, and becomes dry below in the glasse without the least moistnesse, like a black earth, that is caput Corvi, or an earthy dry element, for thus the true sublimation or exaltation of the philosophers is perfected as is said before. And in this sublimation is the true separation of the Elements, as the Masters say.

www.ingramcontent.com/pod-product-compliance
Lightning Source LLC
Chambersburg PA
CBHW071752090426
42738CB00011B/2668